Sky my kids !
Ciel mes enfants !

Du même auteur

La Théière de Chardin
Garnier, 1979

L'Allemaniaque de la France profonde
AMP Éditions, 1981

L'Agenda du VIP
Garnier, 1982

La Khomenie du pouvoir
Scorpio, 1982

L'Album du BCBG
AMP, 1985

Sky my husband ! Ciel mon mari !
Hermé, 1985
Seuil, coll. « Points Actuels », 1987

Le Guide du futur directeur général
avec Marie Garagnoux
Hermé, 1986

Mon carnet secret FM
Carrère, 1986

Les Meilleures Histoires
de bonnes manières
Carrère, 1987

Sky my teacher !
Carrère, 1987

Suites et Fins
Carrère, 1988

Heaume sweet home : dictionnaire illustré
des homonymes franco-anglais
Harraps, 1989

Sky my wife ! Ciel ma femme !
Carrère, 1989
Seuil, coll. « Points Actuels », 1991

Édouard, ça m'interpelle
Belfond, 1990

L'Agenda du Jet Set
Cherche-Midi Éditeur, 1991

Un si gentil petit garçon
Payot, 1992

Le dictionnaire des mots
qui n'existent pas
Presses de la Cité, 1992

Jean-Loup Chiflet

Sky my kids !
Ciel mes enfants !

Dictionary
of branched english

Dictionnaire
de l'anglais branché

DESSINS DE CLAB

Éditions Payot

En couverture : dessin de Clab

ISBN 2-02-015994-5
(ISBN 2-228-88435-9, 1ᵉ publication)

© Éditions Payot, octobre 1991

Remerciements

J'aimerais remercier tout particulièrement ceux qui m'ont aidé à l'élaboration de ce livre, en commençant par mes enfants et leurs amis qui m'ont laborieusement initié au « parler ado ».

Merci aussi à Maggie Doyle, d'origine anglo-saxonne (comme son nom l'indique peut-être), qui a dû arracher courageusement quelques-uns de ses beaux cheveux pour nous aider à trouver les bonnes traductions dans sa langue maternelle.

Merci à Clab, remarquable illustratrice, et ma fidèle complice depuis les tous débuts de l'aventure *sky*.

John Wolf Whistle

Avertissement

Pour ceux qui n'auraient pas encore la chance d'être initiés à la méthode *sky*, voici quelques conseils pour tirer un profit maximum de ces cours d'anglais très particulier.

Le principe de traduction *sky* est très simple : il consiste à traduire une expression ou une phrase française par un mot à mot plus qu'approximatif (c'est un euphémisme !) pour obtenir une phrase anglaise qui ne veut strictement rien dire.

Tous les coups sont permis, l'usage de l'argot en particulier, et surtout une parfaite mauvaise foi dans le choix de la traduction d'un mot lorsque plusieurs significations sont possibles.

Exemple : traduire le mot « Bourse » par « Testicle » et non par « Stock-Exchange » est parfaitement scandaleux mais, je le répète, délibéré : que les lecteurs offusqués s'abstiennent donc de m'écrire pour me dire que je me suis trompé.

Dans le cas très particulier de *Sky my kids !* il s'agit d'obliger les « kids » à pratiquer quotidiennement et dans la joie les rudiments de la langue anglaise — et pour me mettre à la portée de nos chers enfants, je n'ai d'ailleurs pas hésité à saupoudrer légèrement de « verlan » :

ex. femme = meuf

woman = manwo

Parents et pédagogues devront par conséquent veiller, à partir de maintenant, à ce que les onomatopées incongrues

auxquelles ils sont hélas ! confrontés quotidiennement :
« genre ! » « oh ! l'autre » ou « prise de tête » se transforment en « kind! » « oh! the other » et « taken of head ».
Quel immense soulagement pour les géniteurs et précepteurs de ces petits monstres terroristes de notre belle langue française que de les voir se transformer du jour au lendemain en anglophiles avertis...

Enfin, pour améliorer encore le côté éminemment pédagogique de la méthode, les adultes français et anglo-saxons trouveront en italique et en anglais correct la signification la plus fidèle de la phrase « ado-barbare ».

Exemple :

Crasse = Crass	= Traduction du mot
Il m'a fait un plan crasse	= Expression ado
« He made me a map crass »	= Traduction *sky*
He did me a bad turn	= Signification en anglais correct de l'expression ado.

Cet ouvrage n'est donc pas un dictionnaire « français-branché, anglais-branché », mais plutôt un dictionnaire « français-branché = anglais normal » avec en prime (et non des moindres !) le sel d'une traduction mot-à-mot, dite *sky*, dans le but évident de se faire retourner dans sa tombe ce pauvre Shakespeare qui depuis le temps en a peut-être bien besoin...

Good luck !

Jean-Loup Chiflet

A

Accident = *Accident*

Ce mec-là , c'est un vrai accident

«This guy is a true accident»

That guy is a real mess

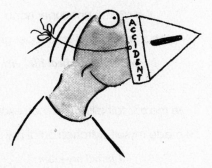

Acier = *Steel*

J'ai un plan d'acier avec une belette

«I have a steel map with a weasel»

I met this girl and I know it's going to work with her

Aller = *To go*

Ça va fort

«It goes strong»

Things are going well

Allumer = *To switch on*

J'ai allumé une super nana

«I have switched on a super girl»

I came on to this beautiful girl

Je me suis fait allumer à mon examen

«I made myself switched on at my exam»

I failed my exam

Angoisse = *Distress*

T'as vu son costume ? C'est l'angoisse

«You saw his suit? It's the distress»

Did you see his suit? It's awful

Arracher = *To tear out*

Je m'arrache, vous me gonflez trop

«I tear me out, since you are inflating me too much»

I'm leaving: you're so boring

Assurer = *To insure*

Ce type assure autant en maths qu'avec les filles

«This guy insures as well in

mathematics as with the girls»

This guy is as good at mathsas he is with girls

Avoine = *Oat*

Mes vieux ne veulent pas me donner d'avoine

«My old don't want to give me oat»

My parents don't want to give me any money

Bague = *Ring*

C'est un mauvais plan : elle est baguée

«Bad map: she is ringed»

It's a pity she's engaged

Bahut = *Cupboard*

Je me suis fait virer du bahut

«I have been turned out from the cupboard»

I have been expelled from school

Baigner = *To bath*

Ça baigne dans l'huile

«It bathes in the oil»

Everything is fine

Balise = *Beacon*

Je balise à mort en avion

«I beacon to death in a plane»

I'm terrified of flying

Baraque = *Shanty*

Cette ordure m'a cassé la baraque

«This garbage has broken me the shanty»

That bastard made me look like a fool

Basket = *Basket*

Cette fille est barbante,

elle ne me lâche pas les baskets

«This girl is bearding, she

does not release me the baskets»

As well as being a pain, that girl never leaves me alone

Bêcher = *To dig*

Tu n'es qu'une sale bêcheuse

«You are just a dirty digger»

You're very haughty

Belette = *Weasel*

Je me suis fait poser un lapin par une belette

«I had a rabbit put down by a weasel»

A girl stood me up

Berge = *Bank*

C'était une vieille peau d'au moins trente berges

«It was an old skin of at least thirty banks»

She was an old woman who was at least thirty

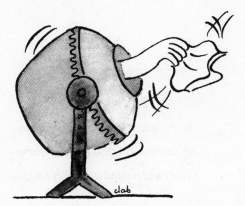

Béton = *Concrete*

Je vais te dire un truc, vaut mieux que tu laisses béton

«I am going to tell you a trick, you better leave concrete»

Believe me, you'd better forget it

Beurre = *Butter*

Ils sont beurrés comme des Petits Lu

«They are buttered like little Lu »

They're plastered

Biche = *Doe*

En roastbeef je biche que dalle

«In roastbeef I doe paving stone»

I can't understand a word of English

Bidon = *Jerrican*

Les "Inconnus" me font vraiment bidonner

«The "Unknown" they really make me jerrican»

The "Inconnus" really make me laugh

Bille = *Marble*

Question bouffe, elle touche pas sa bille

«Question puff, she does not touch her marble»

She can't cook to save her life

Blaireau = *Badger*

C'est pas le mauvais cheval mais c'est un vrai blaireau

«He is not the bad horse but he is a real badger»

He's not a bad sort but he's very stupid

Bleu = *Blue*

Attention ! Voilà les bleus !

«Watch! Here are the blues!»

Watch out! Here come the police!

Bœuf = *Beef*

J'ai tapé le bœuf avec des super musicos

«I have smacked the beef with super musicians»

I jammed with some great musicians

Bol = *Bowl*

J'en ai ras le bol de ces casse-bonbons

«I have it short the bowl of these break-sweet»

I'm fed up with these morons

Bon = *Good*

Parfois c'est bonnard d'en tenir une bonne

«Sometimes it's goodard to hold a good one»

It's nice sometimes to get good and drunk

Bonjour = *Good morning*

Il ne lit que des bédés... Bonjour la culture !

«He only read designed bands...

Good morning the culture!»

He only reads comics: he's not very well read

Botte = *Boot*

J'ai rencontré une nana très chouette.

Elle me botte hyper

«I met a very owl girl. She boots me hyper»

I met this great girl. I really like her

Boudin = *Sausage*

Il a levé un de ces boudins, j'te dis pas !

«He has lifted one of these sausages, I don't tell you!»

He was flirting with this hag!

Bouffi = *Puffy*

Tu l'as dit bouffi

«You have said it puffy»

You'd better believe it

Boule = *Ball*

J'ai les boules avant les exams

«I have the balls before the exams»

I'm scared stiff before exams

Bourre = *Flock*

Ce mec est toujours à la bourre

«This guy is always at the flock»

That guy is always late

J'ai tellement siroté

que j'étais bourré comme un coing

«I have so much siruped

that I was flocked like a quince»

I drank so much I was completely out of it

Bout = *End*

Allez ! On met les bouts

«Go! We put the ends»

O.K.! Let's get out of here

Branche = *Branch*

Je suis plus branché jazz que heavy metal

«I am more branched jazz than heavy metal»

I prefer jazz to heavy metal

Branler = *To swing*

J'en ai rien à branler de ton blé

«I have nothing to swing of your corn»

I'll have nothing to do with your money

Briser = *To smash*

La politique ça me les brise

«Politics it does smash them to me»

Politics bore me to tears

Brosser = *To brush*

Tu peux toujours te brosser

pour t'envoyer en l'air avec elle

«You may always brush you,

to send yourself in the air with her»

You don't stand a chance with her

Brouter = *To browse*

Quand j'en vois des qui prennent

de l'herbe, ça me les broute

«When I see some who take herb,it browses them to me»

I am disgusted by people who smoke dope

Bûche = *Log*

J'ai vachement bûché mon exam et je me suis planté

«I have cowly logged my exam and I planted myself»

I worked very hard for that exam and I failed it

Bulle = *Bubble*

Quand je pense qu'il y en a qui ont

assez de pot pour coincer la bulle

«When I think that there are some who have

enough pot to wedge up the bubble»

When I think there are those who are

lucky enough to have nothing to do

Ça va chier des bulles

«It's going to shit bubbles»

It's going to hot up

C

Cacahuète = *Peanut*

Avec les meufs j'assure pas une cacahuète

«With the menwo I do not insure a peanut»

I don't know how to deal with women

Cageot = *Cageotte*

Si tu voyais le cageot qu'il se farcit

«If you would see the cageotte

that he is stuffing himself»

You should see the witch he's going out with

Cailler = *To curdle*

On se caille les miches !

«One's curdle ones loaves!»

It's freezing!

Came = *Cam*

Ta came c'est vraiment de la daube

«Your cam is real stew»

Your drugs are lousy

Canon = *Gun*

Pendant les vacances j'ai rencontré un mec canon

«During the holidays I have met a gun guy»

I met this gorgeous guy while I was on holidays

Capote = *Overcoat*

J'assure toujours avec mes capotes anglaises

«I always insure with my English overcoats»

To be on the safe side, I always have French letters

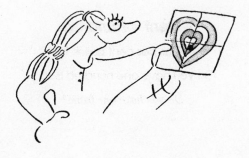

Carton = *Cardboard*

Hier soir en boîte j'ai fait un carton

«Last night in box I made a cardboard»

I picked someone up last night

Casser = *To break*

Aujourd'hui je suis cassé, je suis sorti toute la nuit

«Today I am broken, went out all over the night»

I'm a wreck today: I was out all last night

Cent = *Hundred*

T'as pas cent balles ?

«Do you have one hundred balls?»

Do you have one franc?

Chauffer = *To warm*

Tu commences à me chauffer avec tes trips cul

«You start to warm me with your ass trips»

I'm sick of hearing about your screwing around

Chier = *To shit*

T'es chié ! Tu crains, merde ! T'as sali mon new 501

«You shit ! You fear shit! You have dirty my new 501»

You horrible little shit! You got my new jeans dirty

Cirer = *To Polish*

Édith Cresson en a rien à cirer de la Bourse

«Édith Watercress has nothing to polish of the Testicle»

Édith Cresson doesn't give a damn about the Stock-Exchange

Clair = *Clear*

C'est clair quoi !

«It's clear what!»

It's obvious

Classe = *Class*

Classieux l'appart. avec les poutres app.

«Classious the appart with visible beams»

That's a classy flat with wooden beams

Clou = *Nail*

Des clous !

Nails!

Not likely!

Cool = *Cool*

Mais où tu vas, toi ? Cool, cool Raoul

«But where are you going ? Cool, cool Raoul»

Calm down

Cône = *Cone*

Qu'est-ce qu'il y a dans ton cône ?

Des herbes de Provence ou quoi ?

«What did you put in your cone?

Herbs from Provence or what?»

What's in your joint? Mixed herbs?

Cracher = *To spit*

Je suis allé à un super concert

où ça crachait des masses

«I went to a super concert where it was spitting masses»

I went to a wonderful concert: the music was hot

Craindre = *To fear*

Ça craint, je dirais même plus, c'est craignos

«It fears and I would say even better, it's fearos»

It's very dangerous

Craquer = *To crack*

Cette meuf me fait craquer

«This manwo makes me crack»

I'm crazy about that woman

Crasse = *Crass*

Il m'a fait un plan crasse

«He made me a map crass»

He did me a bad turn

Crèche = *Crib*

En ce moment, je crèche dans un squatt

«These days I crib in a squat»

Right now I'm living in a squat

Crever = *Burst*

J'ai failli me faire crever dans le tromé

«I failed to be burst in the groundunder»

I almost got stabbed in the metro

Crise = *Crisis*

Si ça continue, je vais criser

«If it goes on I am going to crisis»

If this continues I'm going to get angry

Crosse = *Butt*

S'il me cherche des crosses, il va me trouver

«If he looks for butts, he is going to find me»

If he's trying to get me mad, he'll succeed

Cuire = *To cook*

Hier soir, je me suis pris une sacrée cuite

«Last night I got a holy cook»

Last night I got drunk out of my skull

Dalle = *Paving stone*

On crève la dalle dans cette soirée

«One burst the paving stone in this party»

There's nothing to eat at this party

Déchirer = *To tear*

Après ma nuit d'enfer,

je suis complètement déchiré

«After my night of hell,

I am completely torn»

After my wild night, I'm a total wreck

Défoncer = *To knock down*

Elles sont fortes ces tiges, elles me défoncent

«They are strong these stems,

they are knocking me down»

These cigarettes are so strong,

I'm having trouble smoking them

Délire = *Delirious*

C'est pas vrai, tu délires ?

«It is not true, you are delirious?»

It can't be, you're joking

Déménager = *To move*

Dans leur dernier tube, ils déménagent sec

«In their last pipe, they move dry»

They are really very good on their last hit

Destroy = *To destroy*

Il est complètement destroy, ce mec

«He is completely destroyed this guy»

That guy is out of his mind

Dire = *To tell*

Il est arrivé avec une tire ! J'te dis pas !

«He came with a pull! I don't tell you !»

He arrived in this super car, I'm telling you!

Discussion = *Discussion*

C'est cool de taper la discussion entre poteaux

«It's cool to smack the discussion between poles»

It's nice to have a chat among friends

Dur = *Hard*

Dur dur !

«Hard hard!»

It's not easy

Écorcher = *To flay*

Ça t'écorcherait la gueule d'être poli ?

«Would it flay your muzzle to be polite?»

Couldn't you be a bit more civil?

Emballer = *To pack*

Ce soir, je sens que je vais emballer

«Tonight I feel that I am going to pack»

I know I'm going to come on something else tonight

Embrouiller = *To tangle*

Je me suis embrouillé avec des taggeurs

«I tangled myself with taggers»

I had a fight with some taggers

Enfer = *Hell*

Putain ! J'ai vu une meule d'enfer

«Prostitute! I have seen a grinding wheel of hell»

Christ! I saw this incredible motorbike

Enfiler = *To thread*

On s'est enfilé une bonne bouffe

«We did thread a good puff»

We ate an excellent meal

Enfler = *To swell*

T'es qu'une enflure

«You are just a swelling »

You poor creep

Étonner = *To astonish*

Tu m'étonnes, John !

«You astonish me, John!»

I agree with you

Exploser = *To explode*

Je suis explosé de rire

«I am exploded of laugh»

I burst out laughing

F

Farcir = *To stuff*

Mes parents, il faut se les farcir !

«My parents, you have to stuff them!»

You have to be able to put up with my parents

Faux = *Wrong*

Sur ce plan-là, t'as tout faux

«On this map you have everything wrong»

As regards that, you're completely wrong

Fendre = *To split*

Ce livre est fendant

«This book is spliting»

This book is hilarious

Flamber = *To flame*

Les Reebok, c'est vraiment de la flambe

«The Reeboks, it is really flame»

Wearing Reeboks is just showing off

Flan = *Custard*

Elle m'a fait un flan et j'ai poireauté deux heures

«She made me a custard and I leeked two hours»

She lied to me and I waited for her for two hours

Flasher = *Flash*

J'ai complètement flashé sur cette fille

«I completely flashed on this girl»

I'm really interested in that girl

Flipper = *To flip*

Pour mon bac, je flippe total

«For my ferry, I am flipping total »

I'm terrified about my graduation exam

Foie = *Lever*

J'ai les foies d'avoir fait un sac de nœuds

«I have the levers to have made a bag of knots»

I'm afraid I made a mistake

Foire = *Fair*

Il y a une bande d'enfoirés

que je ne peux pas encaisser

«There is a band of enfaired that I cannot cash»

There's a crowd of shits I can't stand

Fouetter = *To whip*

Je fouette car pour mon examen

je crois que les carottes sont cuites

«I whip for my exam because

I think the carrots are cooked»

I'm worried about my exam because I think I've failed

Frire = *To fry*

J'ai failli me friter avec des mecs

qui me prenaient le crâne

«I almost fried myself with guys

who where taking me the skull»

I almost fought with some guys who were getting on my case

Fun = *Fun*

On a passé un week-end outre fun

«We did spend an over fun weekend»

We had a very good time this weekend

G

Gaffe = *Hook*

T'as intérêt à faire gaffe !

«You have interest to make hook!»

You'd better look out!

Galère = *Slave ship*

Tes fêtes à la mords-moi-le-nœud,
c'est toujours des plans galères

«Your feasts at the bite-me-the-knot,
it's always maps slave ships»

Your parties are badly organised and are always a mess

Gamelle = *Kettle*

L'équipe de Bernard Tapie

s'est ramassé une belle gamelle

«The team of Bernard Carpet

picked up a nice kettle»

Bernard Tapie's team had the stuffing knocked out of them

Gaule = *Stick*

J'te raconte pas comment

qu'elle est gaulée, la meuf

«I don't tell you how she is sticked the manwo»

I can't tell you how beautiful that woman is

Gaver = *To cram*

Votre plan boîte, franchement, ça me gave

«Your box map, frankly, it crams me»

I don't want to go out to a night club with you

Gaz = *Gas*

On se boit une Kro vite fait sur le gaz

«Let's drink a Kro quick made on the gas»

Let's have a quick bottle of Kronenbourg beer

Géant = *Giant*

C'est géant ce qu'on a goupillé pour les vacances

«It is giant, what we pinned for the holidays»

We've planned something marvellous for our holidays

Genre = *Kind*

Genre, t'as eu ton bac ?

«Kind, you got your ferry?»

You're certain you got your graduation exam?

Gerbe = *Sheaf*

J'ai la gerbe tellement je mouille

«I have the sheaf so much I wet»

I'm so scared I want to throw up

Gicler = *To squirt out*

Gicle avant que je t'allume la tête

«Squirt out before I switch your head»

Get out of here before I smash your face in

Gland = *Acorn*

Ton frère est un vrai gland

et en plus il n'arrête pas de glander

«Your brother is a real acorn and he never stops to acorn»

Your brother is an idiot and as well as that,

he never lifts a finger

Glauque = *Glaucous*

Dans cette boum, il n'y avait que des gens glauques

«In this party they were only glaucous people»

There were only mournful people at this party

Gluant = *Glummy*

Ce type me chauffe vraiment tellement il est gluant

«This guy warms me a lot so much he is glummy»

That guy annoys me the way he is always hanging around

Gnome = *Gnome*

Ton beau-frère, c'est un vrai gnome

«Your nice brother is a true gnome»

Your brother-in-law is a fool

Grave = *Grave*

Sur la tête de ma mère, tu es grave, toi!

«On the head of my mother you are grave, you!»

I swear you're no good

H

Haine = *Hate*

C'est la haine ! On m'a taxé mon Perf

«It is the hate! One has taxed my Perf»

It's awful! Someone has stolen my leather bomber jacket

Halluciner = *To hallucinate*

Tu hallucines, ou quoi ?

«You hallucinate or what?»

Are you nuts or what?

Honte = *Shame*

J'ai rencontré Sidonie quand j'étais

avec ma vieille, la honte !

«I met Sidonie when I was with my old, the shame!»

I met Sidonie when I was with my mother, I was so ashamed

Huître = *Oyster*

Je ne supporte pas sa face d'huître

«I do not stand his face of oyster»

I can't stand his ugly mug

Incruster = *To incrust*

Ce soir, on va essayer de taper l'incruste dans une fête

«Tonight, we are going to smack the incrust in a feast»

This evening we'll try and crash a party

Jante = *Felly*

Après le certcon, j'étais too much déjanté

«After the certcon, I was too much unfelllied»

After the concert I was totally wound up

Jeter = *To throw*

On a eu le temps de s'en mettre plein
la lampe avant de se faire jeter

«We had time to get ourselves full the lamp
before we were thrown away»

*We had enough time to stuff our faces before
we were thrown out*

Jeton = *Chip*

Il lui a filé un tel jeton qu'il ne savait plus son nom

«He thread him such a chip that he even

didn't remember his name»

He gave him such a punch he couldn't remember who he was

Jurer = *To swear*

Non ? Jure ? Tu ne sors pas avec cette erreur humaine

«No? Swear? You are not going out with this human error»

No? Honest? You're going out with that creep

K . L

Kiki = *Neck*

C'est parti mon kiki

«It is gone my neck»

Here we go

Killer = *Killer*

Ce type, c'est vraiment un killer

«This chap, is a real killer»

That guy is very dangerous

Lâcher = *To drop*

Lâche-moi la grappe, tu me gonfles

«Drop me the cluster, you are inflating me»

Leave me alone, you're bugging me

Laisser = *To Leave*

Laisse béton, c'est pas pour toi, ça coûte la peau du cul

«Leave concrete, it's not for you, it costs the skin of the ass»

Forget it, it's too expensive for you

Larguer = *To release*

Jo la Banane s'est fait larguer par sa meuf

«Jo the Banana has been released by his manwo»

Jo the Banana's wife has left him

Lessiver = *To wash*

Le sport, ça me lessive trop

«The sport, it washes myself too much»

Sport is too tiring for me

Lézard = *Lizard*

Y'a pas de lézard ! C'est du tout cuit

«There is no lizard! It is all cooked»

That shouldn't be a problem, it's very easy

Lourd = *Heavy*

Ça me lourde de rester avec mes vieux

«It heavies me to stay with my old»

Living with my parents is getting on my nerves

M

Main = *Hand*

Prends-toi en mains c'est ton destin !

«Take yourself in your hands, it's your destiny!»

Pull yourself together! You're in control of your future!

Mal = *Bad*

Dis pas ça, tu te fais du mal

«Don't say that, you are making yourself bad»

Don't be so pessimistic

Malaise = *Discomfort*

J'te raconte pas le malaise quand je l'ai vu

«I don't tell you the discomfort when I saw him»

I felt very uncomfortable when I saw him

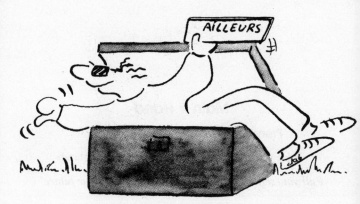

Malle = *Trunk*

On se fait la malle, c'est trop galère ici

«We make the trunk, it is too slave ship here»

Let's get out of here, it's such a bore

Masse = *Mass*

J'ai rarement vu quelqu'un être autant à la masse

«I have rarely seen somebody to be as much at the mass»

I've rarely seen someone that crazy

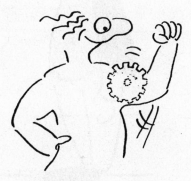

Mécanique = *Mechanical*

Tiens ! Voilà le rouleur de mécaniques qui ramène sa fraise

«Hold! here is the roller of mechanicals

who brings back his strawberry»

Well! here comes that show-off

Mère = *Mother*

Rentre chez ta mère !

«Go back to your mother!»

Piss off!

Morue = *Cod*

A sa place, je n'oserais pas sortir

avec une morue pareille

«In his place, I would not dare to go out with such a cod»

If I were he, I wouldn't dare to go out with that cow

Moule = *Mussel*

J'ai trouvé un giga plan pour les vacances.

J'ai vraiment eu de la moule

«I did found a big map for the holidays.

I really had mussel»

I have a great idea for my holidays. I was really lucky

Mourir = To die

Plus nul, tu meurs

«More zero, you die»

It can't be worse than that

Va mourir !

«Go and die!»

Leave! You're getting on my nerves

N

Neveu = *Nephew*

Je veux mon neveu !

«I want my nephew!»

You bet!

Niveau = *Level*

Au niveau du vécu, ça m'interpelle quelque part

«At the level of the lived, it is something

which call me upon somewhere»

That's something which I find interesting

Nouille = *Noodle*

Pour les examens, il a le cul bordé de nouilles

«For the exams, he has the ass bordered by noodles»

He's always lucky at exams

O.P.Q

Œil = *Eye*

Attention les yeux !

«Be careful the eyes!»

Look out

Or = *Gold*

J'en connais qui se font des couilles en or

«I know some ones who are making

themselves golden testicles»

I know some people who make piles of money

Os = *Bone*

Cette fois-ci, tu l'as dans l'os

«That time, you get it in the bone»

You're screwed this time

Out = *Out*

J'ai trop fumé, je suis out of Africa

«I smoked too much, I am out of Africa»

I smoked too much, I'm stoned

Pâté = *Pie*

Quand je ne dors pas assez,

je suis dans le pâté toute la journée

«When I do not sleep enough, I am in the pie all the day»

When I can't get enough sleep, I'm groggy all day

Patin = *Skate*

J'aimerais bien lui rouler un patin

«I would like to roll her a skate»

I'd like to kiss her (him)

Pêche = *Peach*

En ce moment, j'ai la méga pêche

«I have the super peach at this moment»

I'm in top form at the moment

Pelle = *Shovel*

Ils sont ronds comme des queues de pelle

«They are round like tails of shovel»

They are drunk as skunks

Pet = *Fart*

Face de pet !

«Face of fart!»

You dolt!

Pétard = *Crack*

Après avoir fumé un pétard

j'ai la tête comme une citrouille

«After having smoked a crack

I have the head like a pumpkin»

After having smoked a joint, I'm out of it

Pièce = *Room*

On est pas aux pièces

«We are not at the rooms»

We're not in any hurry

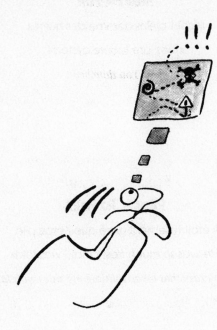

Plan = *Map*

Samedi on a zoné toute la soirée,

c'était vraiment un plan loose

«Saturday we have zoned all the night,

it was truly a map loose»

We wasted our time wandering around on Saturday night

Plein = *Full*

Ils sont pleins comme des huîtres

«They are full like oysters»

They are bombed

Plier = *To Fold*

Il était tellement givré que j'étais plié

«He was so much frosty that I was fold»

He was so crazy that I was splitting my sides with laughter

Plisser = *To Pleat*

Arrête de me chier des pendules, ça me plisse

«Stop to shit me clocks, it pleats me»

Stop bugging me, it gets on my nerves

Poil = *Hair*

On s'est vachement poilé

«We cowly haired ourselves»

We laughed a lot

Pointer = *To point*

Quand elle s'est pointée, j'ai trop halluciné

«When she pointed herself, I was too much hallucinated»

When she arrived I was completely fascinated

Pomme = *Apple*

Je n'aime pas les gens qui se sucent la pomme

«I don't like people who suck their apple»

I don't like people who kiss

Pomper = *To pump*

Tu commences à me pomper l'air

«You start to pump me the air»

You're beginning to annoy me

J'ai rarement vu une nana aussi pompante

«I have rarely seen a girl as much pumping»

I've rarely seen a girl that encroaching

Il marche à côté de ses pompes

«He walks at the side of his pumps»

He's out of his mind

Positiver = *To positive*

Quand la vie c'est cool, je positive

«When life is cool, I positive»

When life is going well, I'm in good form

Potage = *Soup*

Il y a une couille dans le potage. Bonjour les dégâts !

«There is a testicle in the soup.

Good morning the damages!»

There's trouble here. Things don't look good!

Poteau = *Poles*

Je me pointerai avec trois ou quatre poteaux

«I will point myself with three or four poles»

I'll be coming with three or four friends

Poule = *Hen*

Alors ma poule ça gaze ?

«Then my hen it gases?»

How are you doing honey?

Poulet = *Chicken*

Et mon cul, c'est du poulet ?

«And my ass, is it chicken?»

What's it to you?

Pourrir = *To rot*

Manu, il s'est fait pourrir sur 400 mètres avec sa poubelle

«Manu has been rotten on 400 meters with his garbage»

Manu was overtaken in less than 400 m in his old jalopy

Premier = *First*

J'ai vu un film de première bourre

«I saw a film of first flock»

I saw a wonderful film

Prendre = *To take*

Tu me prends le chou

«You take me the cabbage»

You're a pain in the ass

Prise de tête

«Taken of head»

That's a real pain

Pur = *Pure*

Je suis allé à un pur concert

«I went to a pure concert»

I went to a brilliant concert

Purée = *Mashed potatoes*

Purée de ta mère !

«Mashed potatoes of your mother!»

Shit!

Queue = *Tail*

Je n'ai pas la queue d'un

«I have not the tail of one»

I don't have a dime

R

Radar = *Radar*

Avant 11 heures du mat, je marche au radar

«Before eleven in the morn, I walk with the radar»

Before eleven a.m., I'm not awake

Raide = *Tight*

Je me suis enfilé tellement de tequila rapido

que j'suis raide dead

«I thread myself so much tequila rapido

that I am tight dead»

I drank so much Tequila I'm completely gone

Ramer = *To row*

On a ramé comme des bêtes sur ce projet

«We have rowed like beasts on this project»

We worked hard on this project

Rat = *Rat*

Tu n'es qu'un rat tu pourrais me payer un féca

«You are just a rat you could pay me a feecof»

You're so tight-fisted, you could at least buy me a coffee

Réel = *Real*

Quand j'ai vu ça, je ne l'ai pas cru, c'était outre réel

«When I saw that I didn't believe it, it was over real»

When I saw that I just couldn't believe it, it was incredible

Rond = *Round*

J'ai plus un rond, style Armée du Salut

«I have no more round, style Army of Hello»

I have no more money

Rouler = *To roll*

On s'en roule un

«Let's roll one»

Let's smoke a joint

S

Saper = *To sap*

Ce mec est super bien sapé

«This guy is super well sapped»

That guy is really well dressed

Scier = *To saw*

Poivre d'Arvor il est hyper ; il me over scie

«Pepper of Arvor, he is hyper; he over saws me»

Poivre d'Arvor is super; he really impresses me

Sec = *Dry*

Quand je l'ai vu, je suis parti aussi sec

«When I saw him, I left also dry»

When I saw him, I immediately left

Je sèche souvent les cours

«I often dry the courses»

I often skip classes

Secouer = *To shake*

J'en ai rien à secouer de ce pingouin

«I have nothing to shake of this penguin»

I don't want to have anything to do with that man

Serrer = *To squeeze*

Je me suis fait encore serrer par les bleus

«I have been again squeezed by the blues»

I got stopped by the police again

Speed = *Speed*

Speed toi la tête

«Speed your head »

Hurry up!

Stone = *Stone*

Un seul pétard de pakistanaise

et tu es complètement stone

«Only one crack of pakistanese

and you are completely stoned»

One Pakistani joint and you're completely out of it

Style = *Style*

Style ! T'as acheté une nouvelle caisse

«Style! You did buy a new case»

Hey! You bought yourself a new car!

Sucrer = *To sugar*

Ils ont sucré le meilleur morceau du film

«They have sugared the best bite of the movie»

They cut the best bit of the film

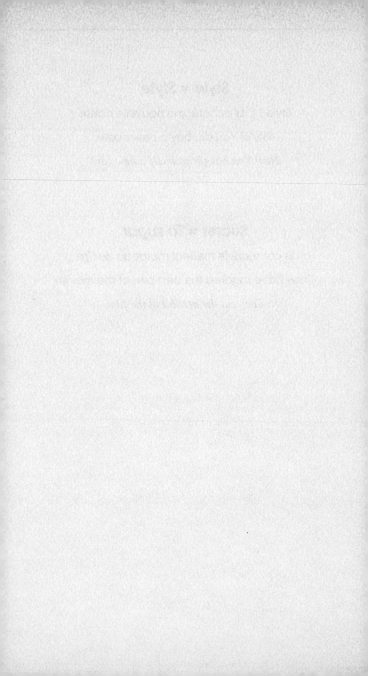

T

Tache = *Spot*

T'es qu'une tache, pistache !

«You are just a spot, pistachio!»

You're a waste of time!

Tailler = *To cut*

On ferait mieux de tailler la route avant l'arrivée des keufs

«We'd better cut the road before the cops arrive»

We'd better get out of here before the cops arrive

Taper = *To smack*

Dans le métro, on se fait toujours taper du blé

«In the tube, we are always being smacked of corn»

You're always being asked for money in the metro

Targette = *Target*

Je me suis fait une targette

«I made myself a target»

I slept with a cow

Taxer = *To tax*

Je lui ai taxé sa voiture

«I taxed his car»

I borrowed his car

Téléphone = *Telephone*

On se téléphone et on se fait une bouffe

«We telephone ourselves and we make a puff»

We'll telephone each other and arrange

to have a meal together

Tente = *Tent*

Il plante sa tente un peu trop souvent

«He plants his tent a little too often»

He invites himself over a little too often

Tête = *Head*

J'ai trop bu hier soir. J'ai la tête dans le cul

«I drank too much last night. I have the head in the ass»

I over drunk last night. I have a hangover

Ça va pas, la tête !

«It's not going the head!»

Are you nuts?

The = *The*

Il croyait que c'était in the pocket et il l'a eu in the baba

«He thought it was in the pocket

and he got it in the baba»

He thought everything was fine and then he was had

Thon = Tuna fish

A force de collectionner les thons,

il pourra faire le Téléthon

«At strong to collect the tuna fishes,

he will be able to make the Telethon»

As a result of going out with all those hags,

he could do a Telethon

Ticket = *Ticket*

Il a un ticket d'accord,

mais on dirait Simone de Beauvoir

«He has a ticket OK, but she looks like

Simone of Nice See»

O.K, so she likes him, but she looks like Simone de Beauvoir

Tirer = *To shoot*

Je me tire, j'ai rancart à Marcadet-Poissonnière

«I shoot myself, I have an appointment
at Marcadet-Fishmonger»

I'm off! I'm meeting someone at Marcadet-Poissonnière

Toile = *Linen*

Ce soir, je me ferais bien une toile

«Tonight, I would make me well a linen»

I'd like to see a film this evening

Tôle = *Sheet iron*

Je me suis tôlé en moto et à mes examens

«I sheet ironed in motorbike and at my exams»

My motorbike crashed and I failed my exam

Touriste = *Tourist*

Ce type, c'est vraiment Jo le Touriste

«This guy is really Jo the Tourist»

That guy is a good for nothing

Tracer = *To trace*

J'me trace, j'rentre à Juvisy-sur-Orge

«I am tracing myself, I go back to Juvisy on Barley»

I'm leaving, I'm going back to Juvisy-sur-Orge

Tranche = *Slice*

J'en ai rien à secouer de cette tranche de cake

«I have nothing to shake of this slice of cake»

I've nothing to do with that fool

Travail = *Work*

Et voilà le travail

«And here is the work»

Here we are! It's finished

Trip = *Trip*

J'suis allé à une soirée ; j'ai bien tripé

«I went to a party where I well tripped»

I went to a party and had a fun time

Tronc = *Trunk*

Je ne veux plus me casser le tronc pour toi

«I don't want to break me the trunk for you»

I don't want to put myself out for you

Trop = *Too much*

Ce gamin est trop

«This child is too much»

What a lovely child!

Trou = *Hole*

Arrête d'enculer les mouches, ça me troue

«Stop to sodomise the flies, it holes me»

It really bugs me when you split hairs

Truand = *Crook*

Si ça se trouve, tu t'es fait truander

«If it finds you make yourself crooked»

It may be that you were conned

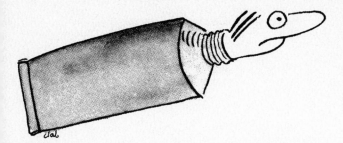

Tube = *Tube*

Je me suis fait entuber de dix sacs

«I made myself intubed of ten bags»

I was robbed of hundred francs

V

Valise = *Suitcase*

Bordel à queue ! T'es con comme une valise

«Bordello at tail! You are as stupid as a suitcase»

Christ! You are so dumb!

Vanne = *Sluice*

Faut pas charrier, j'étais juste en train de te vanner

«Do not carry, I was just in train to sluice yourself»

Don't get mad I was only teasing!

Venir = *To come*

Viens chez moi, j'habite chez une copine

«Come at my place, I live at a girlfriend's place»

Come to my place, I live at my girlfriend's

Vinaigre = *Vinegar*

Si tu veux être à l'heure, tu dois faire vinaigre

«If you want to be at the hour, you must do vinegar»

If you want to be on time, you'd better hurry

Vingt = *Twenty*

Vingt-deux, voilà les keufs !

«Twenty two, here are the cops!»

Watch out! Here come the cops!

Viser = To Point

Vise un peu la meuf, on dirait Carole Bouquet

«Point a little the manwo, she looks like Carole Bunch»

Look at that woman, she's just like Carole Bouquet

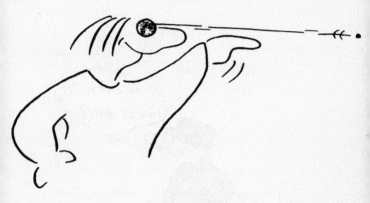

Voile = *Sail*

J'en connais un qui est à voile et à vapeur

«I know one who is at sail and steam»

I know someone who swings both ways

Z

Zéro = *Zero*

Quand je vais chez le médecin, je les ai à zéro

«When I go to the doctor, I have them at zero»

I'm terrified when I go to the doctor's

Zone = *Zone*

Chez toi c'est vraiment la zone

«At your place it is really the zone»

Your place is a pigsty

IMPRIMERIE BRODARD ET TAUPIN À LA FLÈCHE (5-93)
DÉPÔT LÉGAL AVRIL 1993. Nº 15994-2 (6040H-5)

Collection Points

SÉRIE ACTUELS